The Sculpture and Drawings of

ELIE NADELMAN

WHITNEY MUSEUM OF AMERICAN ART, NEW YORK

September 23–November 30, 1975

HIRSHHORN MUSEUM AND SCULPTURE GARDEN
SMITHSONIAN INSTITUTION, WASHINGTON, D.C.

December 18, 1975–February 15, 1976

An Exhibition Organized by the Whitney Museum of American Art

The Sculpture and Drawings of

ELIE NADELMAN

1882-1946

SPONSORS

This exhibition was made possible by generous grants from the Helena Rubinstein Foundation and the National Endowment for the Arts.

The Helena Rubinstein Foundation is dedicated to the advancement of the public good especially in those areas with which its founder was closely identified during her lifetime. It is particularly fitting that the first full-scale retrospective of Nadelman's work should be sponsored by the Foundation, since Mme Rubinstein was one of the artist's earliest and most generous patrons. When, in 1911, he held a one-man exhibition at Paterson's Gallery in London, she bought the whole show. And it was Mme Rubinstein who helped him emigrate in 1914 to the United States, where she lent him her garage in Rye to assemble his first New York exhibition. Many of the works in this exhibition were at one time in her collection.

Text by John I. H. Baur
Chronology by Hayden Herrera

FOREWORD AND ACKNOWLEDGMENTS

IT IS HARD TO IMAGINE what would have happened to Elie Nadelman's reputation without Lincoln Kirstein. It was he who wrote the catalogue of the first retrospective exhibition of Nadelman's work at the Museum of Modern Art in 1948, two years after the artist's death. Within the next year he had published a book on Nadelman's drawings and an article on his dance subjects.[1] In 1973 there appeared his definitive monograph on Nadelman,[2] which is not only the most exhaustive study of his work and life, but surely one of the most remarkable books of its kind in the thoroughness with which it investigates the events and influences that form an artist, his stylistic development, his relation to the social forces of his time and his own influences on others.

It would be impossible to summarize all past findings here. To anyone seriously interested in Nadelman's work, prior monographs are essential. In the following pages I have tried to do four things: to give a personal view of Nadelman's position in American art, to clarify his stylistic growth, to make the facts of his career more easily available through the Chronology which Hayden Herrera has compiled; finally, to illustrate, in addition to the better known works, several which were not shown at the Museum of Modern Art and a number which are not reproduced in either catalogue or monograph. Research for this exhibition has turned up a number of these which were either unlisted or noted as "lost" in Mr. Kirstein's "Draft Catalogue Raisonné."

Neither this exhibition nor its catalogue would have been possible without the generous assistance and advice of two other persons: E. Jan Nadelman, the artist's son, who has lent extensively to the exhibition and has helped in a great number of ways, and Dr. Athena T. Spear of Oberlin College, whose scholarly research on Nadelman's early work has cleared up many difficult problems of dating and stylistic evolution. Not only were her two articles extremely helpful,[3] but she has also responded generously to inquiries on individual pieces.

The cooperation of the Hirshhorn Museum and Sculpture Garden was another vital factor in the organization of the exhibition. Joseph Hirshhorn's private collection of Nadelman's work was the largest anywhere outside the artist's family, and most of it went to the museum that bears his name. The director, Abram Lerner, and the curator, Mrs. Lawrence McCabe, responded generously to the project at its inception, making all the Museum's works available and aiding the undertaking in many other ways. It seems particularly appropriate, therefore, that the exhibition could be shown at the Hirshhorn Museum as well as at the Whitney.

A special word of gratitude must be expressed to Virginia Zabriskie and her assistant Suzanne Vanderwoude. In organizing two Nadelman exhibitions at the Zabriskie Gallery in 1967 and 1974, they assembled much information on the artist's work and its present location, which they shared most generously. I am also deeply indebted to the many museums, galleries and private collectors who lent their works to the exhibition.

Finally, a word about the exhibition itself: with 103 sculptures and 41 drawings it is over twice the size of the 1948 show at the Museum of Modern Art (which had 44 sculpture entries and an unnumbered group of drawings). It does not include prints, nor did the earlier show. It is more representative of Nadelman's diverse interests since it includes portraits, neoclassical works, decorative pieces and a very large selection of those *Ideal Heads* into which he poured so much energy. All of these were either absent from or scantily represented in the 1948 survey.

A number of major works are exhibited or reproduced here for the first time since Nadelman's death nearly thirty years ago, among them the bronze *Female Nude* (no. 51), the four unusually large terra-cottas of *The Four Seasons*[4] (nos. 36–39), two important marbles, i.e., the broken, unfinished but still beautiful *Seated Woman* (no. 64) and the *Female Nude* (no. 52). Together with other slightly better known works, these enlarge, I believe, our understanding of Nadelman's range and the creative diversity of his art.

John I. H. Baur

INTRODUCTION

ELIE NADELMAN was in love with style. It is the central fact in his life and in his art. While he had predilections for various subjects at various times, his true concern, as he made clear in a much-quoted statement in *Camera Work* (October 1910), was formal: "The subject of any work of art is for me nothing but a pretext for creating significant form, relations of forms which create a new life that has nothing to do with life in nature, a life from which art is born, and from which spring style and unity."

Style and unity: the wonder is how any unity emerged from the number of historic styles which influenced Nadelman at various times and from the diverse manners in which he himself worked, often simultaneously. Yet a unity did emerge, for there is an underlying Nadelman character in everything he did.

His sources were protean. Before he left Paris in 1914 at the age of 32, he was apparently affected by Rodin, perhaps by the 15th-century carver Viet Stoss, by the drawings of Aubrey Beardsley, by Greek sculpture of both the Hellenistic period and 5th century B.C., by the Art Nouveau of Obrist, Adolph Von Hildebrand's neoclassicism, Michelangelo's *Bound Slaves*, the mannerism of Giovanni da Bologna, the sculpture of Clodion and Houdon, the drawings of Constantin Guys and the paintings of Seurat. In the United States after 1914, he was plainly entranced with folk art—of which he was an early collector—and with many kinds of popular art such as movies, jazz, dancers, circus performers, vaudeville figures and the concert stage. Tanagra figurines were influential on his last work.

Nor is this catalogue complete, for there are individual Nadelman pieces that show his passing awareness of such art as the prehistoric cave drawings at Lascaux, and of various specific works of antiquity. It is enough, however, to heighten one's conviction that Nadelman was a deliberate connoisseur of style—an eclectic who borrowed creatively, never slavishly, from an astonishing number of historic and contemporary modes of expression.

Nadelman's own variations in style are almost as numerous as his sources. Athena T. Spear (see footnote 3) identifies eight drawing styles (which she labels with the letters A through H) and four styles in his figure sculptures during the brief period 1905–12. The Spear classification of the drawings is based largely on technical variations (relation of shading to line, etc.) and need not be recapitulated here. On broader stylistic grounds there are perhaps three different drawing manners—first a proto-cubist style in which a series of heads are analyzed in quasi-geometrical volumes (nos. 104, 105), second and most prevalent, a linear style of intersecting curves, arcs and sinuous lines, with or without shading (e.g., no. 109), third and rarest, an almost baroque style of vibrating light and shade (e.g., no. 113).

Nadelman himself saw his early drawings in simpler terms. In the same *Camera Work* statement of 1910, quoted above, he wrote: "I employ no other line than the curve, which possesses freshness and force. I compose these curves so as to bring them in accord or opposition to one another. In that way I obtain the life of form, i.e., harmony."

Later in his career his drawings explored other directions. A lively and often humorous quality informed his cows (no. 128) and poodles (no. 130) and birds (nos. 108, 138). In some heads the drawing became fanciful and calligraphic (no. 129), in others grotesque (no. 134). But as a graphic artist he never surpassed the vitality of the drawings done in Paris before 1912.

To some extent Nadelman's early sculpture parallels the styles of the drawings, though with significant differences. Dr. Spear divides his figure sculptures into four groups: first, the female nudes of classical inspiration; second, the "monstrous nudes" of the Venus Pudica type; third, the "tubular" mannered figures; and fourth, the Cubist mannered figures. Nadelman's early heads fit predominantly into the first of these categories, though some are scattered in the last two.

Following for the moment this classification, it is apparent that, numerically at least, the neoclassical vein was the strongest. Not only are there a number of female nudes based on the proportions and poses of Greek antiquity (nos. 1, 2, 8, 30), but literally dozens of idealized marble heads ring every conceivable change on the Greek profile with its leptorrhine nose, its sharply chiseled lips, its rhythmically repeated patterns of hair. These heads are far from the chilly neoclassical formulas of Canova or Thorvaldsen; in spite of their obvious debt to Greek art they are unmistakably contemporary in feeling. The subtle volumes, the nearly abstract harmony of forms make them more a tribute to the classical spirit than an imitation of its style.

But Nadelman was not content to stay within the limits of the Greek canon. What Dr. Spear calls the "monstrous nudes," such as the one sometimes known as *Gertrude Stein* (no. 6), appear to have been a deliberately anticlassical treatment of a classical theme. Similarly, the tubular mannered style appears to have been an experiment in simplifying classical figures far beyond the limits observed in Greek antiquity (nos. 9, 25). It is as if Nadelman was playing with the whole concept of solid sculptural form by turning it into liquid volumes that flow into each other—a method he revived more emphatically in his late work.

But it is in the so-called Cubist mannered works that Nadelman made perhaps his greatest innovations at this period. As early as 1908 he had done a curvilinear Cubist head which Picasso saw and which certainly influenced the French artist's own sculpture of the following year. Nadelman himself dated his experiments with Cubist analysis of form back to drawings he did in 1905, and in later years was bitter at not being recognized as a founder of Cubism. Sifting the evidence, Lincoln Kirstein concludes that Nadelman's claims of precedence are just but that his understanding of Cubism was not profound and his influence on the movement not extensive.

In themselves, however, Nadelman's mannered figures and heads, in which the forms approached geometrical abstraction, are both compelling and his farthest reaction against Greek art. Often the heads are schematic, eyes and mouths are slits (nos. 3, 5) or the eyes become half spheres with noses and eye sockets defined as sharply tilted planes (nos. 4, 21). The figure pieces are even more extreme in geometry and proportion. Muscles swell into curved protrusions and are echoed in out-thrust hips (nos. 14, 15). A head is sometimes reduced to the size of a pea (no. 7). Breasts become hemispheres and drapery a swirling decoration over the starkly simplified architecture of the body, as in *Draped Standing Female Figure*. This is a piece which Nadelman did in wood (not in the exhibition), in dark bronze (no. 13) and in bright polished bronze (no. 12)—a translation into various media which he often repeated throughout his career, apparently feeling that form was the important consideration, the material less so.

In addition to the styles analyzed by Dr. Spear, Nadelman began, while still in Paris, to develop a decorative manner of fluid lines and great elegance. This is apparent in the first version of his *Horse* (no. 31), probably done about 1911, and in a series of figures (*Four Seasons*, nos. 36–39) and reliefs (no. 35) which he did for Helena Rubinstein.

It is a style half way between mannerism and classicism, an exotic expression which seems quintessentially Nadelman in its cool detachment and its aura of nostalgia for the past. Like so much of his work it is more a celebration of style than a use of style as a means to an end.

After Nadelman came to America in 1914, his work evolved in different directions, though he never totally abandoned his early preoccupations. His decorative work found its first expression in a series of animals—especially stags and does (nos. 45–48), done soon after his arrival, and as late as about 1930 he produced a fountain (no. 91) of great decorative vitality.

He also returned over and over to the classicism of his early figures and ideal heads, although a softer modeling, a slight blurring of the separate parts is now noticeable. Two large *Female Nudes* (nos. 51, 52) are witness to the major effort he still expended on his interpretation of Greek ideals in the teens (although possibly done just before he left France), while another nude *Figure* (no. 79) of about 1925 is a final echo of his pure neoclassicism. Predominantly classical, too, though with overtones of Cubism, are his *Dancing Figure* (no. 60) and *Female Dancer* (no. 72), both probably done close to 1920.

The extreme mannerism of Nadelman's pre-American years waned in this country, but his early tubular style (which had, as we noted, manneristic elements) went through a number of variants and was the base from which most of his American work evolved. His first major piece here, *Man in the Open Air* (no. 43), is almost pure tubular style, mannered, fluid, invincibly elegant. But in the tree, the hat and the bow tie Nadelman introduces a new element, a contemporary note, a bare suggestion that this is a modern dandy in an actual setting, not a classical or idealized figure (although the classical allusions are plain enough). It presages the series of wood and plaster figures which followed in the next few years and by which he is perhaps best known today.

These charming scenes of contemporary life were done, from 1916 to 1919, in a new manner which resulted from the modification of his tubular style by the influence of American folk art. That Nadelman should be affected by our naive artists, then little appreciated, was not so strange in itself; both Robert Laurent (about 1916) and William Zorach (about 1917) were aware of folk art and utilized some of its directness and expressive qualities in their sculpture. Its reevaluation was just beginning and Nadelman was only one of several artists who understood its esthetic qualities.

But it was in combining folk art elements with his own tubular style that Nadelman proved his creative ingenuity. His stylistic instinct took precisely what was needed from both and created a new style—not a pseudo-primitivism but a sophisticated, fluent, urbane way of commenting on those aspects of society which engaged him. It was as though he had understood the inner impulses of the folk artist—to record as directly as possible what is familiar and loved—and had preserved its artless spontaneity within the framework of his own sophisticated vision.

In a series of plaster pieces (all destroyed) and carved wood figures done probably in the years 1916–19, Nadelman explored his own cherished aspects of America—a woman at the piano (no. 59), dancers (no. 65, 71), circus performers (nos. 67, 68), an orchestra conductor (no. 69), society figures, male and female, seated in elegantly spare metal chairs (nos, 63, 70). These he often produced in two or three nearly identical versions with the aid of paid assistants, although there is no firm evidence of the sequence in which the different versions were done.

Closely related stylistically to these wooden pieces are two unusual works in other media, *Sur La Plage* (no. 55) in marble and bronze—the only work in which Nadelman mixed these materials—and the unfinished marble *Seated Woman* (no. 64), which despite its broken arms is one of the most graceful of all his clothed ladies, poised and delicate. The marble nude of *Sur La Plage* is even more elegantly fluid. She harks back to the tubular nudes of his Paris days, but the contemporary elements in the scene relate the piece more closely in feeling to the wooden groups, which it apparently preceded.

If Nadelman had worked, in America, only in the directions we have discussed—the decorative, the neoclassical, the tubular-folk art—he would still be remembered as an artist of wide ranging styles. But his appetite for formal innovation was great and led him in still other directions almost diametrically opposed to the controlled forms, the fluid, linear profiles, the mannered elongations which are the hallmark, in varying degree, of all the above work.

Before going to Paris Nadelman had done some expressionist sculpture halfway between Rodin and Barlach.[5] While he never returned to this manner he did experiment again, about 1915, with expressionist distortions in two small sculptures of bulls (nos. 49, 50), which are the antithesis of the sleek stags and does he was creating at the same time. The rough and lively surfaces reflect light in a Rodin-like, impressionist way, although Lincoln Kirstein suggests that they were probably more influenced by the cave drawings of Lascaux than by the French master.

It was not a direction Nadelman followed, but it presages his drift away from classicism which began some ten years later and grew in strength during the last twenty years of his life. Not that he ever abandoned completely the classical ideals which had been so strong in his early work. He had made from these a series of personal styles which, as we have seen, absorbed at various times elements of Cubism, of folk art and of mannerism. What bound these diverse styles together was not so much the echo of Greek art (though that could be sensed occasionally), but an underlying devotion to classicism in its wider formal sense—as opposed to romanticism—an esthetic of clarity, measure, flowing contours, and a concept of the whole as a harmonious sum of clearly defined parts.

Yet no great artist is totally classical or totally romantic—as Sir Kenneth Clark has often pointed out. The seeds of anticlassicism were always present in Nadelman; they had sprouted briefly in his early Rodinesque work, in the extreme mannerism of pieces like the *Draped Standing Female Figure* (nos. 12, 13) which seems to strain against classical bounds in an almost baroque way, and, of course, in the *Bulls.*

About 1924 Nadelman modeled a series of large figures (e.g., no. 73) in a medium he called galvano-plastique (plaster covered by a thin electroplating of metal), some of which were later cast in bronze (nos. 74, 75). These still emphasize flowing contours in a way that may be called classical, but something very strange happened to the interior forms, that is, to the parts. They have melted. It is no longer possible to define a breast, a shoulder, a hip; it is even hard to say where legs and arms begin. Details of the face are deliberately blurred. The whole work becomes a single undulating volume. The total effect is more baroque than classical, although no precedent in past art exists for these extraordinary, boneless figures.

Nadelman carried this "veiled style" (it is hard to think of a better word for it) even further in several busts of which *Bust of a Woman* (no. 78) is perhaps the most extreme example. Here even the contour—last vestige of classicism in the big figures—has ceased to function esthetically. The piece is an inchoate shape in which features of the face—eyes, nose, mouth, chin—seem to struggle vainly to emerge from the surface veil that obscures everything except where the most prominent forms have pushed it out.

For several years Nadelman experimented in this vein, sometimes returning to sharper contours and clearer details—as in *Man in a Top Hat* (no. 80) or the *Bust of a Woman (Henrietta Stettheimer ?)* (no. 81), both of about 1926–28—but eventually coming back, as if fascinated, to the mysterious and amorphous forms of the galvanos. He tried carving these veiled figures in marble (no. 83), modeling them in terra-cotta (no. 87) and papier-mâché (no. 85). Often, when a woman holds a dog or a child in her lap (nos. 89, 92) it is difficult to distinguish the two figures from each other.

Finally, about 1930–31, Nadelman modeled in plaster, covered with paper, two five-foot-high pairs of women which were later cast in bronze (nos. 91, 95) and still later enlarged in marble for the Promenade of the State Theater in Lincoln Center. In these his blurred style reached its fullest expression and justified itself by the extraordinary unity and monumentality he achieved. They look, each pair, like Siamese twins inextricably joined, as if growing out of each other. But since they are plainly goddesses, not mortals, nor even individualized, we accept the distortion and indeed forget it in the powerful flow of forms that ripple without stop across the heavy masses. Here Nadelman achieves a unity that he had sought in his tubular nudes of twenty years earlier, and in the big galvanos of the twenties, but with a new assurance.

From the mid-thirties to his death in 1946, Nadelman produced no large works. In a few carved heads such as the *Charles Baudelaire* (no. 100) and *Head of a Woman* (no. 99), he recaptured some of the clarity and classical feeling of his earlier work, although the softness of his blurred style still invades these like a subtle mist, obscuring details and emphasizing the masses of the heads rather than their features.

But Nadelman's most significant late work was a series of tiny figures in plaster (no. 101), a few of which were posthumously cast in bronze (nos. 102, 103) and terra-cotta. Apparently his object in these was to produce them from plaster molds at a price the public could afford, and, as Kirstein points out, he may have been influenced in this by the popular Tanagra figurines of Greek antiquity, which also plainly influenced the form of some of his own small figures.

Yet many of these—perhaps the majority—are very far from the graceful, attenuated forms of the Tanagra pieces. With heads and shoulders too large for their delicate legs and feet, they seem top-heavy in proportion, sometimes baleful in appearance. While they often appear to be dancing, their motions are not those of ballet or ballroom; they are more like maenads driven by mysterious inner frenzy. Doll-like, unreal, they haunt the imagination.

Stylistically, these little figurines mark the final evolution of Nadelman's blurred style, but with expressionist overtones that are absent from the big galvanos. Instead of flowing contours and large, harmoniously proportioned masses, we now have fretted and broken outlines, radical distortions of features and of proportions. Despite the distant echo of Tanagra, they are the most anticlassical, the most romantic and baroque of all Nadelman's work. They close his career on a wild, dark note which may have expressed the personal trials he suffered at the end of his life—his fortune wiped out in the Depression, his kiln and studio gone, his folk art collection dispersed, his reputation as an artist in eclipse. But they are not an expression of defeat—more of escape, or perhaps defiance.

Looking back on Nadelman's work, nearly thirty years after his death, his contribution to modern sculpture in America looms ever larger. While many of our painters took part in the modernist revolutions in Europe from very nearly their beginnings and even launched avant-garde movements of their own, such as Synchromism, our sculptors were more conservative. Before 1920, William Zorach and Robert Laurent experimented rather cautiously with both expressionist distortion and semiabstract simplifications of form, but they moved rapidly in more traditional directions. Their principal concern became the revival of direct carving with its attendant esthetic of the expression of the material, the release of the form sensed in a boulder or a log, the open expression of the artist's carving technique by means of toolmarks left on the stone. None of this was necessarily antithetical to modern formal concepts, but in practice it worked out that way. Certainly the direct carvers would have been horrified by Nadelman's use of paid assistants to do much of his preliminary carving, just as Nadelman could not have understood a preoccupation with materials and methods taking precedence over formal considerations.

The only American sculptor, before 1920, who rivaled Nadelman in formal innovations and creative vigor was Gaston Lachaise. But Lachaise's sexual imagery, bursting forms and linear vitality were very different from Nadelman's cooler and more intellectual art. Nor did Lachaise exert much influence on the American scene until after his first one-man shows in 1918 and 1920.

Nadelman, on the other hand, came to America in 1914 as an already famous artist, his circle of artist friends was wide and his influence pervasive. Even the more academic sculptors admired him, including Frederick MacMonnies, Mahonri Young, Paul Manship, Gertrude Vanderbilt Whitney and George Grey Barnard. Kenneth Hayes Miller once told Nadelman, "We all go by what you do," and artists as diverse as George Bellows, Eugene Speicher and the caricaturist John Held, Jr., were among his admirers.

The precise nature of Nadelman's influence is harder to assess. Apparently his decorative style, particularly as expressed in his animals, affected both Manship and Hunt Diedrich. His ideal heads have a brief echo in a few similar heads by Lachaise, although the latter generally individualized his subjects more. (It is also possible that the influence flowed in the other direction, and that Lachaise's *Equestrienne* of 1918 may have been in Nadelman's mind when he did his *Woman on Horse* of c. 1935.)

But Nadelman's influence was both deeper and less specific than these instances. It was perhaps less stylistic than intellectual. His passion for form, for the relations of curves and volumes was manifest, and it came at a time when America had been shaken by the revolutionary aspects of Cubism and Fauvism and was reassessing the aims of art. But by 1920 even our avant-garde painters were retreating from pure abstraction, which began to seem like a dead end, and were trying to find a way to combine the formal values they had learned in Paris and Munich with subjects drawn from American life. Nadelman's art, particularly his wooden genre pieces, showed a way to do this. Their influence is immediately apparent in the paintings of Guy Pène du Bois and perhaps in the radical simplifications of Rockwell Kent, particularly his illustrations. It is less apparent in the semiabstract designs of the Precisionists (artists like Charles Sheeler, Charles Demuth, Niles Spencer, Georgia O'Keeffe) probably because they seldom treated the human figure, while Nadelman dealt with almost nothing else. But the intellectual basis for Precisionism—its emphasis on abstract design, on the suppression of detail, on simple volumes—is close to Nadelman's esthetic philosophy, whether it derived from it or not.

Only after 1930 when Nadelman largely withdrew from art circles and started his lonely voyage into the world of those blurred and distorted dolls of his last years did his influence wane. A comparable sculpture of fantasy and distortion did not appear again in America until the small late bronzes of Jacques Lipchitz in the 1950s and '60s.

But, needless to say, the ultimate value of an artist is not measured by his influence on others, although that has its historical importance. It is measured by our sense of value in the individual vision and individual touch of hand which make his work different from that of others. While Nadelman ranged through many styles, his cool, elegant, even aristocratic way of looking at form and the unmistakable handwriting that he placed on everything he touched seem always inevitably and totally his. He was a passionate intellectual, aware of his own position in the evolution of western art, a position that comprised all he valued from the past and all he savored in the present.

FOOTNOTES

1. Lincoln Kirstein, *Elie Nadelman Drawings*, New York, 1949, reprinted 1970. Lincoln Kirstein, "Elie Nadelman: Sculptor of the Dance," *Dance Index*, 7, no. 6 (1948): 131–51.

2. Lincoln Kirstein, *Elie Nadelman*, New York, 1973.

3. Athena T. Spear, "Elie Nadelman's Early Heads (1905–1911)," *Allen Memorial Art Museum Bulletin*, Oberlin College, 28, no. 3 (1971): 201–22. Athena T. Spear, "The Multiple Styles of Elie Nadelman: Drawings and Figure Sculptures ca. 1905–12," *ibid.*, 31, no. 1 (1973–74): 34–58.

4. One of these was listed in the 1948 exhibition and two were illustrated in the catalogue; the other two have been seen only by visitors to the offices of Helena Rubinstein, Inc.

5. Two pieces, done about 1903, are reproduced in the second article by Athena T. Spear cited in footnote 3.

CHRONOLOGY

1882	February 20, Elie Nadelman born in Warsaw, Polish Russia, seventh child of Hannah Arnstam and Philip Nadelman. Father a jeweler; mother's family included artists, writers and musicians.
c. 1887–99	Attended Warsaw's Gymnasium and High School of Liberal Arts.
c. 1899	Briefly attended Warsaw Art Academy.
1900–01	Volunteered for the Imperial Russian Army as an officer candidate. Taught drawing and flute to officers' children.
c. 1901	Returned to Warsaw Art Academy for one year.
c. 1902	Went to Cracow for two days, but returned to continue study in Warsaw. Won prize in *Sztuka* magazine's annual competition for memorial to Fréderic Chopin.
1904	To Munich for six months. Saw antique dolls in Bavarian National Museum, and classic Greek sculpture in Glyptothek. Possibly influenced by work of Aubrey Beardsley, Herman Obrist, August Endell and Adolf von Hildebrand. Admired Munich's circus, opera and music halls. Arrived in Paris late in year. Drew briefly from model at Atelier Colarossi, without criticism. Affected by visits to Louvre where he made drawings after Michelangelo's sculpture. Also influenced by Rodin and Seurat. Took studio in a courtyard behind 14 Avenue du Maine off the rue de Vaugirard.
1905–07	Exhibited in Salon d'Automne. From 1906–14 the only titles Nadelman gave his analytical drawings were "Rapports des Formes" or "Recherches des Volumes." Exhibited in Salon des Indépendants (1907) and with Berthe Weill, rue Victor Massé.
1908	Leo Stein took Picasso to Nadelman's studio, where Nadelman's head of a man, c. 1907, may have influenced Picasso's bronze *Head* of 1909. Stein bought several drawings and a plaster nude. (See no. 6.)
1909	April 25 or 26, first one-man show opened at Galerie Druet, Paris. Exhibition great success. After a vacation near Dieppe, moved to larger studio at 15 rue de Boissonade. Began carving a series of classical female heads.

1910	*Camera Work* (no. 32, October) published statement by Nadelman defining his concept of abstraction in terms of "significant form."
1911	Exhibited in Barcelona with Manolo. Saw bullfights and prehistoric cave paintings in the Dordogne, which inspired his later sculptures of bulls. To London for one-man show in April at Paterson's Gallery. Helena Rubinstein bought entire exhibition.
1912	Marinetti's lecture on Futurism at Bernheim-Jeune Gallery caused fight when Nadelman took issue with his denunciations of the art of the past.
1913	January, exhibited at non-jury salon, Berlin. Purchased by German collectors. February, exhibited twelve drawings and a plaster male head, c. 1908 (destroyed), at the Armory Show, New York. June, second Paris exhibition at Galerie Druet.
1914	Publication in Paris of *Vers L'Unité Plastique*, a portfolio of about 50 facsimiles of drawings (reissued in 1921 in New York as *Vers la Beauté Plastique*). March, first serious article on Nadelman by André Salmon, published in *L'Art Decoratif*. From c. 1914 on, Nadelman was concerned with ironically simplified depictions of contemporary social types. Summer spent near Ostend. At outbreak of war, went to Russian Embassy in Brussels to enlist as reservist in Russian Army, but was informed of impossibility of crossing Europe. Reached London, and, with help of Helena Rubinstein, obtained passage to U.S.A. October 31, arrived in New York City.
c. 1914–15	Took studio on West 14th Street. Martin Birnbaum, connoisseur, critic and junior partner at Scott & Fowles, visited Nadelman's studio. Birnbaum made arrangements for exhibition, and prepared article on Nadelman for *The International Studio*, December 1915. Marble head by Nadelman given to Rhode Island School of Design, his first work to enter a museum. (Within next five years, Nadelman's work was acquired by at least six other museums.)
1915–16	December to January, first exhibition in New York at Stieglitz's Photo-Secession Gallery ("291") included a plaster version of *Man in the Open Air* (no. 43).
1917	February, Scott & Fowles exhibition, New York, a near sellout. After exhibition, Nadelman vacationed with Helena Rubinstein and her family at Greenbrier, White Sulphur Springs, West Virginia. December, Allies of Sculpture exhibition, Ritz-Carlton Roof, New York, organized by a group of society women as war charity. Nadelman showed four plaster figures, including *La Femme Assise* (no. 63). Taken as satire, because of contemporary costume, it caused a scandal. Was removed from the exhibition for three days, then, because of publicity, replaced, but in an unobtrusive corner. Finally knocked off its pedestal and broken. Nadelman's defense of his figures in contemporary dress appeared in three newspapers. February 3, *New York Times* announced Nadelman's engagement to Miss Judith L. Bernays. Engagement later broken.
1919	October 27–November 8, exhibition at M. Knoedler & Co., New York, of 16 sculptures and 40 drawings, including *Woman at the Piano* (no. 59), *Dancer* (no. 65), *Orchestra Conductor* (no. 69), and *Host* (no. 70). Exhibition not well received, and neither plasters nor wood versions of them were sold until after his death. Married Mrs. Joseph A. Flannery.

1920	The Nadelmans purchased Alderbrook, an estate at Riverdale, and a town house at 6 East 93rd Street. At about this time Nadelman set up a studio-shop with three assistants, including Albert Boni, his *practicien* from Paris. Turned out editions of up to six wood or bronze figures. Nadelman became friend of Stettheimer sisters. He appears in Ettie Stettheimer's novel, *Love Days* (1923), and a polychromed bronze bust (no. 82) is probably of her. From early 1920s, Nadelmans collected folk art. In 1923–28 they spent over half a million dollars on their collection.
1921	Summer, rented Henry Sleeper's home in Gloucester, Massachusetts, famous for period rooms.
1924–26	Built museum on Riverdale estate to house folk art collection.
1925	Showed galvano-plastiques for first time in March at Scott & Fowles and May 1–June 4 in a one-man exhibition at The Arts Club of Chicago. Wrote letter to Henry Goddard Leach, editor of *The Forum*, for a symposium on "Is Cubism Pure Art," in which he asserted the importance of his influence on the genesis of Cubism and his priority over Picasso.
1926–28	Did series of busts in painted bright bronze, e.g., *Man in Top Hat* (no. 81).
1926–33	Traveled to Europe during four summers (1926, 1927, 1928, 1933).
1927	One-man exhibitions January 31–February 12 at M. Knoedler & Co., New York, and May 23–June 27, Galerie Bernheim-Jeune, Paris. Became American citizen, sponsored by Eugene Speicher.
1929	Forced by financial losses to rent, then sell Manhattan house. By 1930 Nadelmans had moved to Alderbrook.
1929–33	Received two architectural commissions from architectural firm Walker and Gilette, one for Fuller Building on 57th Street and Madison, the other for the Bank of the Manhattan Company, Wall Street.
1930	September 23–October 13, last one-man exhibition during lifetime at Galerie Bernheim-Jeune, Paris. Thereafter stopped exhibiting and sold little, although he continued to work intensively.
1930–35	Had kiln and experimented with ceramics. Became increasingly interested in producing large editions of small sculpture. Experimented with small papier-mâché figures done in editions from plaster molds. Did no more bronze or wood sculpture, but carved about a dozen small marbles.
1935	Sold studio together with kiln. Worked mainly in Plastilene, making small figures which he cast in plaster from molds.
c. 1935–37	Folk art collection sold, together with the building which housed it. In 1937, Nadelman wrote to a friend, "the dismantling of the Museum did also dismantle something in me."
1942	February, enrolled in Riverdale Air Warden Service. In spite of bad heart condition, took late night and early morning watches. Volunteered to instruct in occupational therapy at Bronx Veterans' Hospital, where he worked for two years teaching ceramics and modeling to wounded soldiers.
1946	December 28, died.

NOTES ON THE CATALOGUE

The sequence is chronological. Dimensions are in inches, height preceding width. In the case of sculpture, only height is given (except for reliefs) and the base is not included unless it is an integral part of the piece. When no lender is listed, the work is lent by Mr. and Mrs. E. Jan Nadelman, New York. Works marked by an asterisk (*) are exhibited at the Whitney Museum only. Works marked by a dagger (†) are not illustrated.

Dates should be accepted with caution, since Nadelman rarely dated his work and kept no records. Dates before 1912 are generally those ascribed by Athena T. Spear, after 1912 by Lincoln Kirstein. However, some dates have been changed when new evidence or the judgment of the author indicated a more likely period.

SCULPTURE

1. *Suppliant.* c. 1905. Bronze, 57 h.

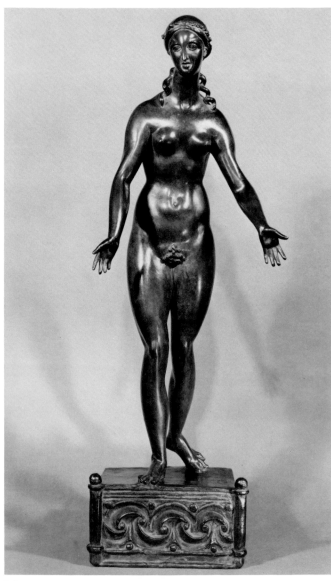

[2]

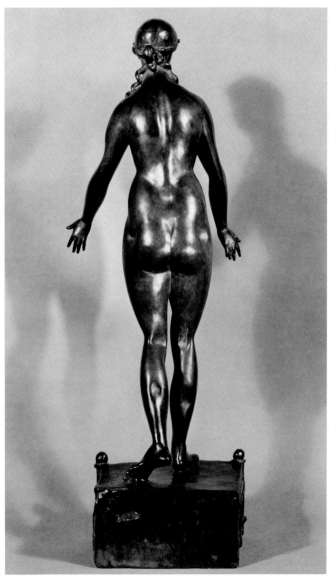

[2]

2. *Standing Female Nude*. c. 1906–07. Bronze, 25 ½ h. Lent anonymously.

3. *Head of a Boy*. c. 1906–07. Gilt bronze, 16¾ h. Lent anonymously.

4. *Ideal Head*. c. 1906–07. Wood, 13 ¾ h. Lent by Sue and David Workman, New York.

[4]

[3]

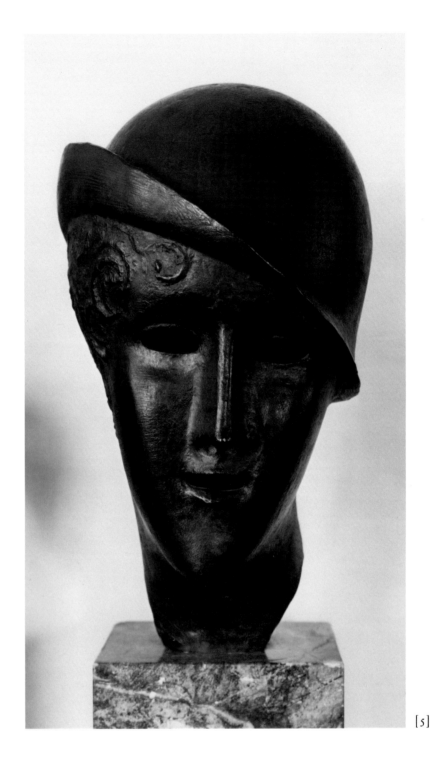

[5]

5. *Man's Head*. c. 1906–07. Bronze, 16 h.

6. *Standing Female Figure* (also called *Gertrude Stein*). c. 1907? Bronze, 29½ h.

[7]

7. *Standing Female Nude*. c. 1907–08. Wood, 15 h. Lent by
   Mr. and Mrs. Monte Getler, New York.

8. *Two Standing Nudes*. c. 1907–08. Gilt bronze, 20½ h.
   Lent by Joslyn Art Museum, Omaha, Nebraska.

[9]

[11]

9.   *Standing Female Figure*. c. 1908. Gilt bronze, 28 h. Lent by Robert Schoelkopf Gallery, New York.

10.   *Classical Head*. c. 1908. Marble, 12½ h. Lent by Miss Mala Rubinstein, New York. (†)

11.   *Woman's Head*. c. 1908. Marble, 17½ h.

12.   *Draped Standing Female Figure* (also called *Recherche des Formes*). c. 1908. Bronze, 23 h. (ILLUS. P. 28)

13.   *Draped Standing Female Figure* (also called *Recherche des Formes*). c. 1908. Bronze, 23 h. Lent courtesy Larcada Gallery, New York. (ILLUS. P. 29)

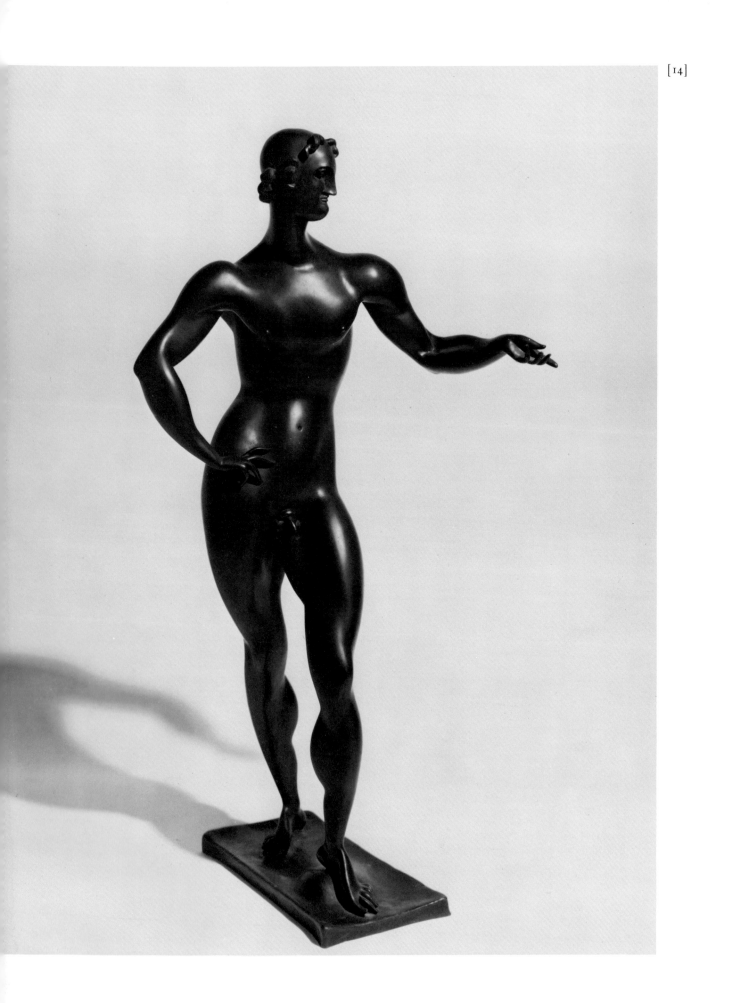

14. *Standing Male Nude.* c. 1908–09. Bronze, 26 h. (ILLUS. P. 30)

15. *Standing Female Nude.* c. 1908–09. Bronze, 26 h. Lent by Hirshhorn Museum and Sculpture Garden, Smithsonian Institution, Washington, D.C. (ILLUS. P. 31)

16. *Classical Head with Headdress.* c. 1908–09. Marble, 14 h. Lent by Zabriskie Gallery, New York.

17. *Classical Head with Headdress.* c. 1908–09. Marble, 4¾ h. Lent by Bella and Sol Fishko, New York.

18. *Classical Head.* c. 1909. Marble, 12⅜ h. Lent by Hirshhorn Museum and Sculpture Garden, Smithsonian Institution, Washington, D.C.

[17]

[18]

19. *Ideal Head.* c. 1909. Wood, 15 h. Lent by Dr. and Mrs. Samuel C. Karlan, New York.

20. *Female Head.* c. 1909. Marble, 14 h. Lent by Allen Memorial Art Museum, Oberlin College, Ohio.

21. *Relief of a Head.* c. 1909. Wood, 14¼ × 9½. (ILLUS. P. 36)

22. *Classical Head.* c. 1909–10. Marble, 6¼ h. Lent by Hirshhorn Museum and Sculpture Garden, Smithsonian Institution, Washington, D.C. (ILLUS. P. 36)

23. *Head of a Woman.* c. 1909–10. Marble, 18 h. Lent by Hirshhorn Museum and Sculpture Garden, Smithsonian Institution, Washington, D.C. (ILLUS. P. 37)

[20]

[25] [25]

24. *Semi-Seated Tubular Nude*. c. 1909–10. Wood, 16 h. Lent anonymously.

25. *Head*. c. 1910. Marble, 13 ¼ h. Lent anonymously.

[27]

[27]

26. *Ideal Head*. c. 1910. Marble, 13 h. Lent by Mr. and Mrs. Maurice Vanderwoude, Great Neck, New York. (ILLUS. P. 42)

27. *Ideal Head*. c. 1910. Marble, 12¾ h. Lent by Mr. and Mrs. Oscar Kolin, New York.

28. *Ideal Head*. c. 1910. Marble, 16 h. Lent by Mr. and Mrs. John D. Mack, Concord, Massachusetts. (†)

29. *Ideal Head*. c. 1909–11. Marble, 8 h. Lent by Mr. and Mrs. Louis S. Myers, Akron, Ohio. (ILLUS. P. 42)

30. *Classical Figure*. c. 1909–11. Marble, 34¾ h. Lent by Hirshhorn Museum and Sculpture Garden, Smithsonian Institution, Washington, D.C. (ILLUS. P. 43)

[29]

[26]

31. *Horse.* c. 1911. Bronze, 36¼ h. (Posthumous cast.)

32. *Man's Head* (also called *Mercury Petassos*). c. 1911. Marble, 12 h. Lent by Miss Mala Rubinstein, New York.

33. *Man's Head* (also called *Mercury Petassos*). c. 1911. Marble, 12½ h. Lent by Miss Mala Rubinstein, New York.

[31]

[32]

[33]

[34]

34. *Ideal Female Head.* c. 1911. Wood, 16 h.

35. *Spring.* c. 1912. Bronze relief, 47× 57× 1½. Collection Whitney Museum of American Art.

36. *Four Seasons, I.* c. 1912. Terra-cotta, 31 h. Lent by Helena Rubinstein Inc., New York.
    (ILLUS. P. 48)

37. *Four Seasons, II.* c. 1912. Terra-cotta, 29¾ h. Lent by Helena Rubinstein, Inc., New York.
    (ILLUS. P. 48)

38. *Four Seasons, III.* c. 1912. Terra-cotta, 30½ h. Lent by Helena Rubinstein, Inc., New York.
    (ILLUS. P. 49)

39. *Four Seasons, IV.* c. 1912. Terra-cotta, 30½ h. Lent by Helena Rubinstein, Inc., New York.
    (ILLUS. P. 49)

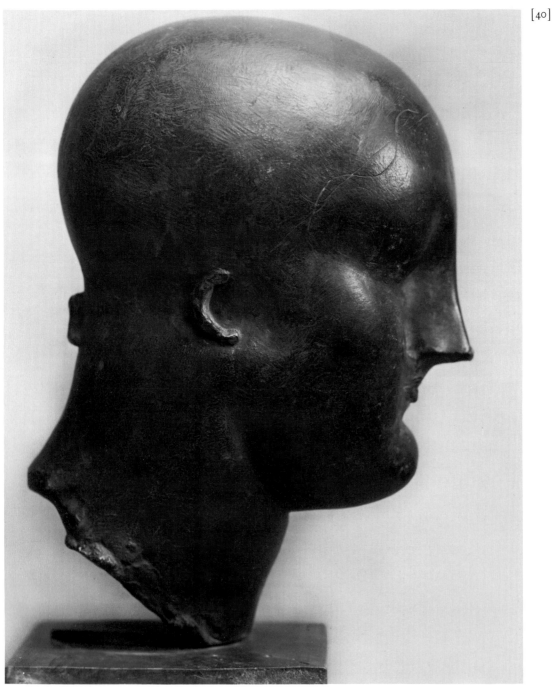

[41]

40. *Male Head*. c. 1911–13. Bronze, 15½ h. Lent by Hirshhorn Museum and Sculpture Garden, Smithsonian Institution, Washington, D.C.

41. *Figure Study*. c. 1913. Bronze relief, 12¼ × 6⅛. Lent by Hirshhorn Museum and Sculpture Garden, Smithsonian Institution, Washington, D.C.

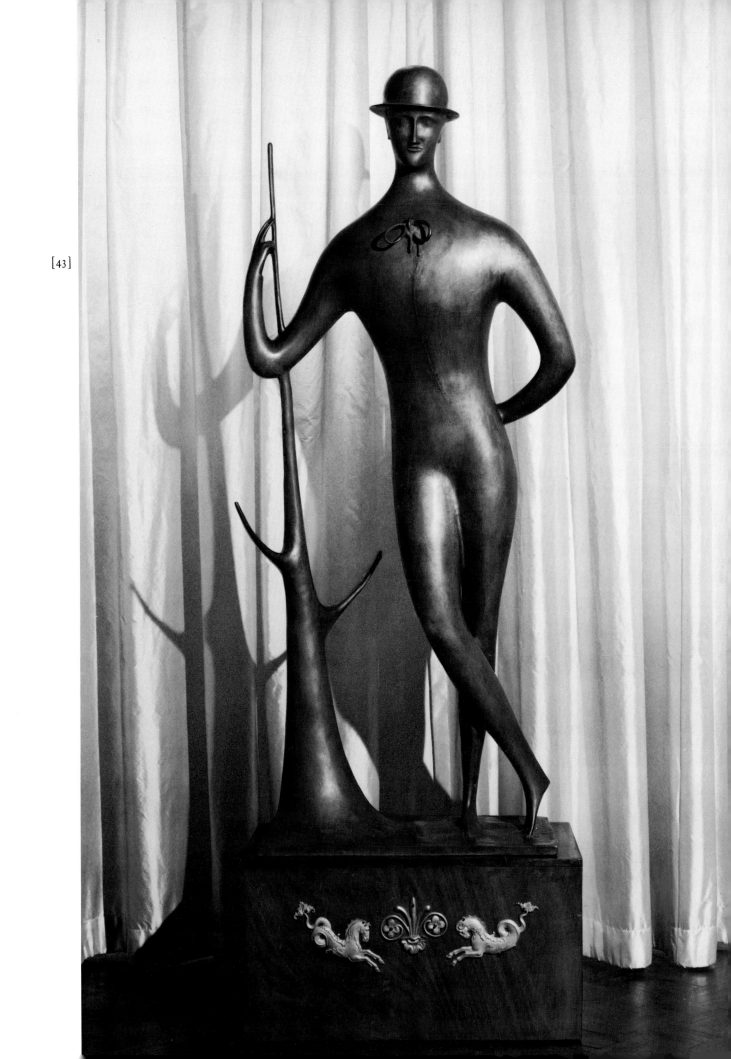

42. *Horse.* c. 1914. Bronze, 12¾ h. Lent by Hirshhorn Museum and Sculpture Garden, Smithsonian Institution, Washington, D.C. (ILLUS. P. 52)

43. *Man in the Open Air.* c. 1914–15. Bronze, 54½ h. Lent anonymously. (ILLUS. P. 53)

44. *Horse and Hounds.* c. 1914–15. Bronze relief, 8¾ × 11¼. Lent by Robert Schoelkopf Gallery, New York. (ILLUS. P. 56)

45. *Doe with Lifted Leg.* c. 1915. Bronze, 20½ h. Lent by The Fine Arts Museums of San Francisco; Hélène Irwin Fagan Collection.

46. *Buck Deer.* c. 1915. Bronze, 29⅞ h. Lent by The Fine Arts Museums of San Francisco; Hélène Irwin Fagan Collection.

[45]

[44]

[47]

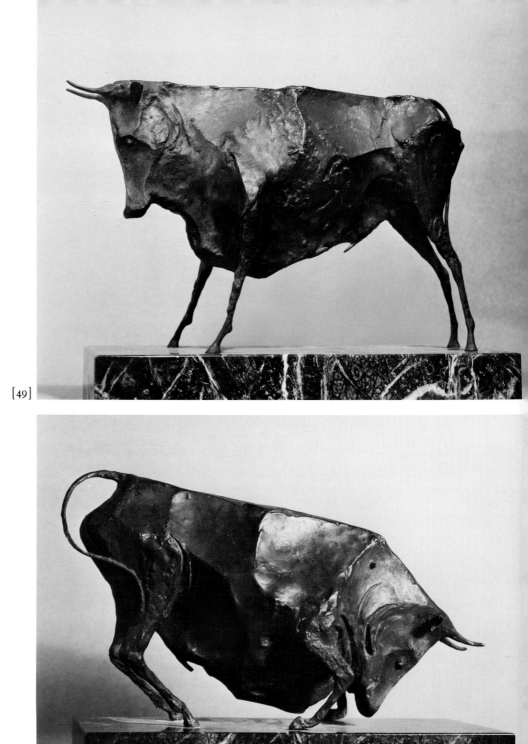

[49]

[50]

47. *Wounded Stag.* c. 1915. Bronze, 13 h.

48. *Resting Stag.* c. 1915. Bronze, 17½ h. Lent by Henry P. McIlhenny Collection, Philadelphia. (†)

49. *Standing Bull.* c. 1915. Bronze, 6⅝ h. Lent by The Museum of Modern Art, New York; Gift of Mrs. Elie Nadelman, 1947.

50. *Wounded Bull.* c. 1915. Bronze, 5⅞ h. Lent by The Museum of Modern Art, New York; Gift of Mrs. Elie Nadelman, 1947.

51. *Female Nude.* c. 1916–20? Bronze, 53 ½ h. (Damaged.) (ILLUS. P. 58)

52. *Female Nude.* c. 1916–20? Marble, 42 ½ h. (ILLUS. P. 59)

53. *Goddess.* c. 1916. Marble, 22 ⅞ h. Lent by The Cleveland Museum of Art; Bequest of James Parmelee.

[57]

[56]

54. *Portrait of a Little Girl* (*Marie Scott*). 1916. Marble, 30 h. Lent by The Metropolitan Museum of Art, New York; Gift of Mrs. Stevenson Scott. (ILLUS. P. 64)

55.* *Sur la Plage.* 1916. Marble and bronze, 23⅜ h. Lent by Sara Roby Foundation, New York.

56. *Acrobat.* c. 1916. Bronze, 13½ h.

57. *Male Head* (*Ideal Self-Portrait?*). c. 1916. Marble, 14½ h. Lent anonymously. (ILLUS. P. 61)

58. *Portrait of Hélène Irwin Fagan* (*Mrs. Templeton Crocker*). 1917. Marble, 29 h. Lent by The Fine Arts Museums of San Francisco; Hélène Irwin Fagan Collection. (ILLUS. P. 65)

[60]

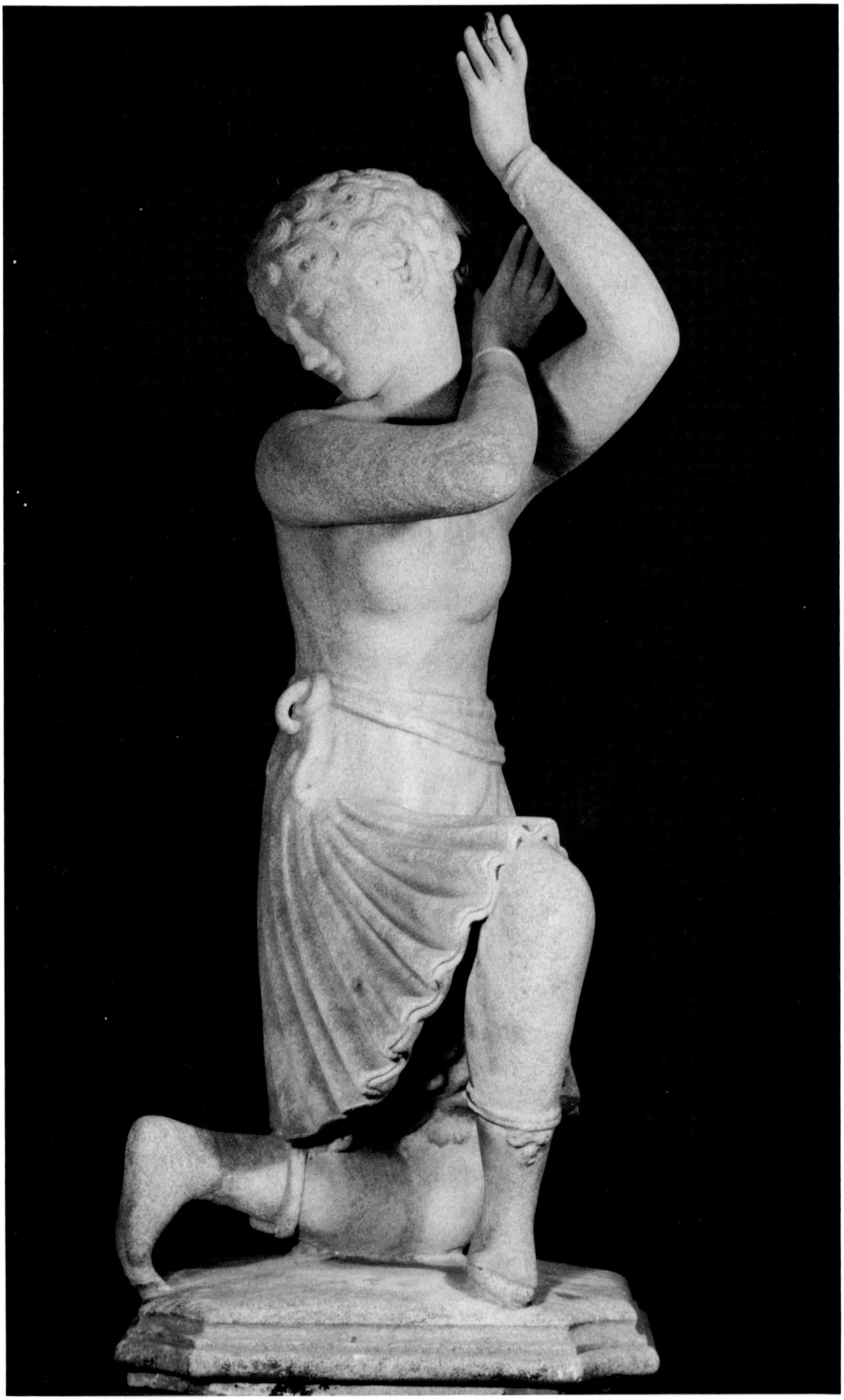

59. *Woman at the Piano (Femme au Piano)*. c. 1917. Stained and painted wood, 35 ⅛ h. (The piano is a restoration.) Lent by The Museum of Modern Art, New York; Philip L. Goodwin Collection, 1958. (ILLUS. P. 68)

60. *Dancing Figure* (also called *Artemis*). c. 1916–18? Marble, 42½ h. Lent by Chrysler Museum at Norfolk, Virginia; Gift of Walter P. Chrysler, Jr.

61. *Chanteuse*. c. 1918. Painted cherry wood, 37 h. Lent by Lloyd Goodrich, New York. (ILLUS. P. 69)

62. *Head of a Woman*. c. 1915–19. Wood, 14½ h. Lent by Mr. and Mrs. Roy V. Titus, New York. (†)

63. *La Femme Assise*. c. 1918–19. Cherry wood and wrought iron, 33 h. Lent anonymously. (ILLUS. P. 71)

64. *Seated Woman*. c. 1918–19. Marble, 34⅜ h. (Unfinished, broken.) (ILLUS. P. 70)

65. *Dancer*. c. 1918–19. Painted cherry wood, 28¼ h. Lent by Wadsworth Atheneum, Hartford, Connecticut; Philip L. Goodwin Collection. (ILLUS. COVER AND P. 72)

66. *Hostess*. c. 1918–19. Painted cherry wood, 32½ h. Lent by Hirshhorn Museum and Sculpture Garden, Smithsonian Institution, Washington, D.C. (ILLUS. P. 73)

67. *Circus Girl*. c. 1919. Painted wood, 31 h. Lent by Hirshhorn Museum and Sculpture Garden, Smithsonian Institution, Washington, D.C. (ILLUS. P. 74)

68. *Circus Performer*. c. 1919. Painted wood, 33½ h. Lent by Hirshhorn Museum and Sculpture Garden, Smithsonian Institution, Washington, D.C. (ILLUS. P. 75)

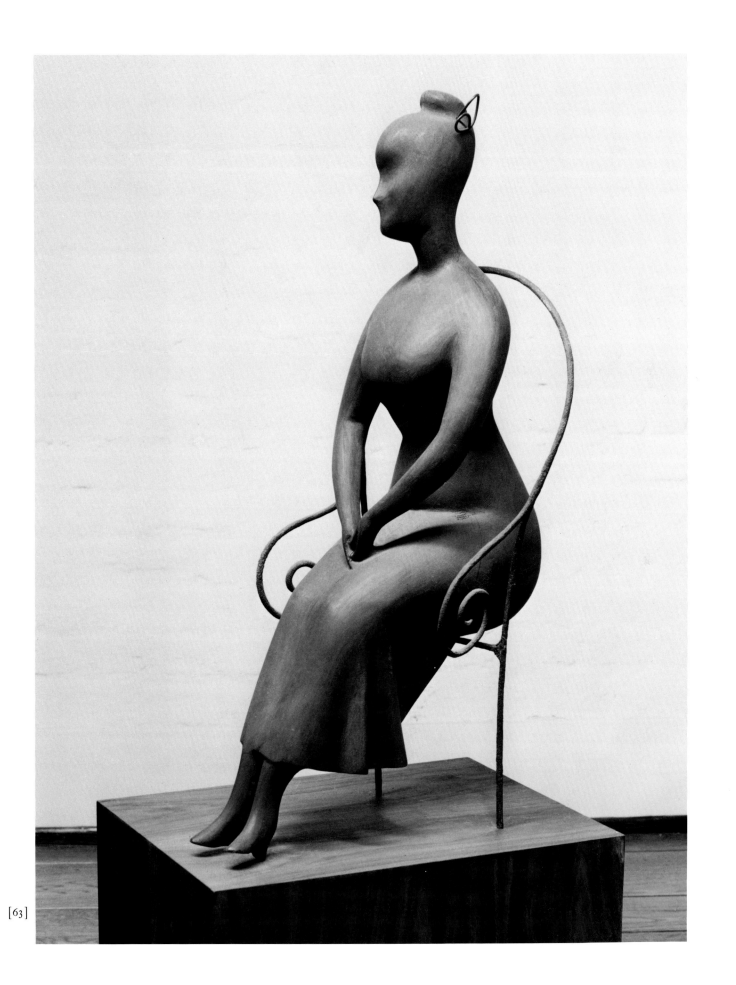

69. *Orchestra Conductor (Chef d' Orchestre)*. c. 1919. Painted cherry wood and gesso, 38½ h. Lent by Hirshhorn Museum and Sculpture Garden, Smithsonian Institution, Washington, D.C.

70. *Host*. c. 1919. Painted cherry wood, gesso, and wrought iron, 28½ h. Lent by Hirshhorn Museum and Sculpture Garden, Smithsonian Institution, Washington, D.C.

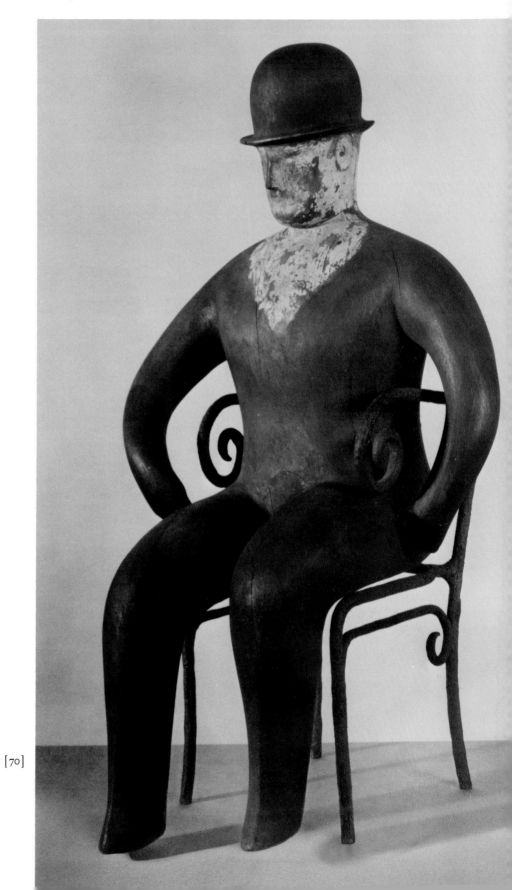

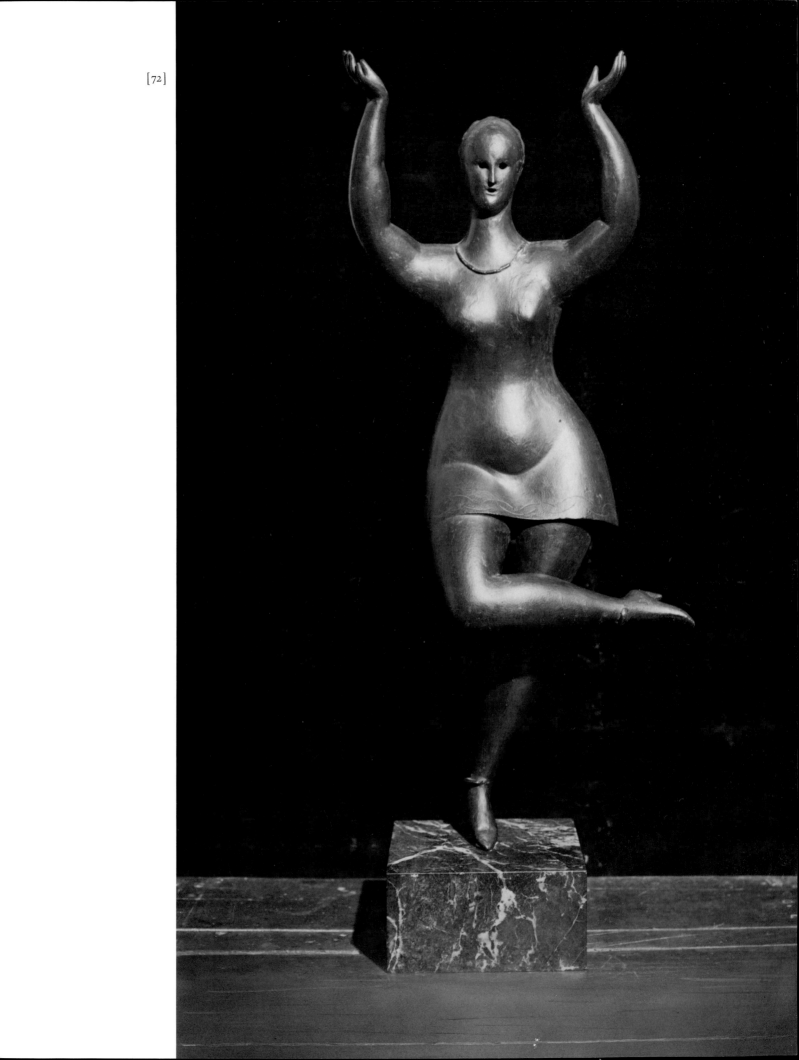

[73]

71. *Tango*. c. 1919. Painted cherry wood and gesso, 34 h. Lent anonymously. (ILLUS. P. 78)

72. *Female Dancer*. c. 1920. Bronze, 32½ h. (ILLUS. P. 79)

73. *Standing Female Figure*. c. 1924. Galvano-plastique, 59½ h.

74. *Seated Woman*. c. 1924. Bronze, 47½ h. (Cast from galvano-plastique, 1964.)

75. *Seated Female Figure*. c. 1924. Bronze, 47 h. (Cast from galvano-plastique, 1964.)

76. *Head of Man in Top Hat*. c. 1924. Painted galvano-plastique, 26¾ h. (†)

77. *Relief Portrait of a Woman*. c. 1920–25. Marble, 28×20. (ILLUS. P. 84)

78. *Bust of a Woman*. c. 1924–25. Galvano-plastique, 26 h.

[77]

[82]

79. *Figure.* c. 1925. Marble, 37½ h. Lent by Walker Art Center, Minneapolis.

80. *Man in a Top Hat.* c. 1927. Painted bronze, 26 h. Lent by The Museum of Modern Art, New York; Abby Aldrich Rockefeller Fund, 1948. (ILLUS. P. 87)

81. *Bust of a Woman (Henrietta Stettheimer?).* c. 1926–28? Painted bronze, 23⅝ h. Lent anonymously. (ILLUS. P. 86)

82. *Portrait of Robert Sterling Clark.* c. 1928. Bronze, 15¼ h. Lent by Sterling and Francine Clark Art Institute, Williamstown, Massachusetts.

83. *Seated Woman.* c. 1928–30. Marble, 6½ h. (†)

84. *Seated Woman* (three versions). c. 1930. Papier-mâché, 4½ h. (Two polychromed and glazed.) (†)

85. *Girl with Poodle.* c. 1930. Papier-mâché, 12½ h.

86. *Woman Dressing Another's Hair.* c. 1930. Papier-mâché, 14¼ h.

87. *Two Women.* c. 1930. Terra-cotta, 16¼ h. (†)

88. *Two Acrobats.* c. 1930. Glazed polychromed ceramic, 10¾ h. Lent by Hirshhorn Museum and Sculpture Garden, Smithsonian Institution, Washington, D.C.

[89]

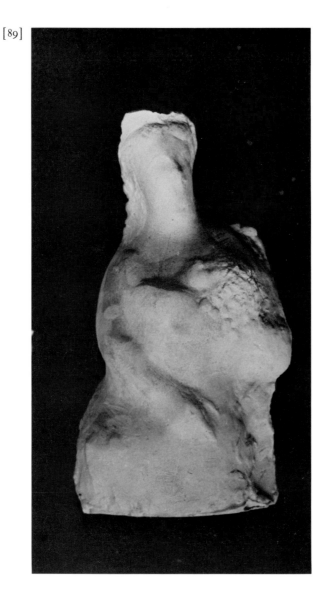

89. *Woman with Child.* c. 1930. Terra-cotta, 7 h.

90. *Two Circus Women.* c. 1930. Bronze, 62½ h. (Posthumous cast from plaster.) Lent by Nelson A. Rockefeller, New York.

91. *Boy and Fish Fountain.* c. 1930? Bronze, 36 h. (ILLUS. P. 92)

92. *Girl with Poodle.* c. 1931. Glazed polychromed ceramic, 7 h. (ILLUS. P. 93)

93. *Standing and Seated Women.* c. 1931. Glazed polychromed ceramic, 16½ h. (†)

94. *Two Female Nudes.* c. 1931. Bronze, 59 h. (Posthumous cast from plaster.) Lent by Nelson A. Rockefeller, New York. (ILLUS. P. 94)

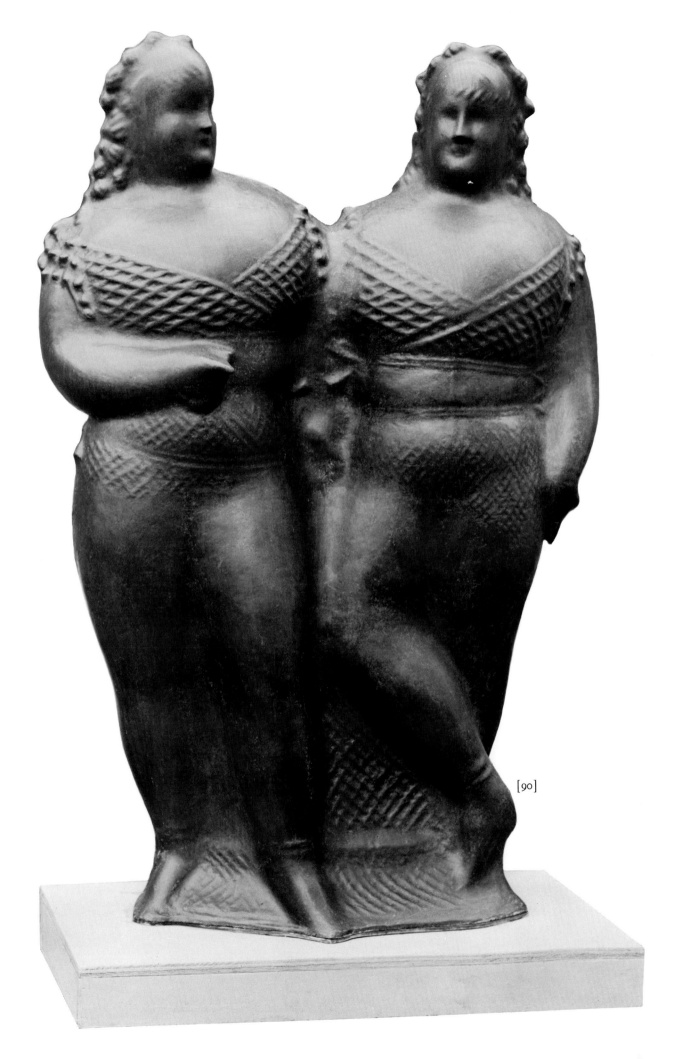

[90]

[92]

[99]

[98]

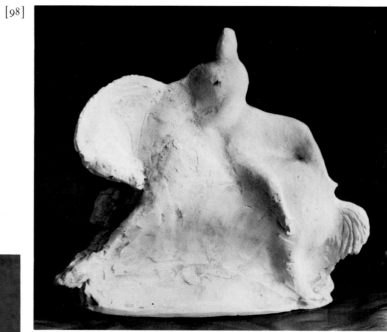

[95]

96

95. *Two Women.* c. 1931. Papier-mâché, 15¾ h.

96. *Standing Woman, I.* c. 1930–35. Marble, 12 h. Lent by Mrs. G. Macculloch Miller, New York. (†)

97. *Standing Woman, II.* c. 1930–35. Marble, 12 h. Lent by Mrs. G. Macculloch Miller, New York. (†)

98. *Woman on Horse.* c. 1935. Plaster, 7 h.

99. *Head of a Woman.* c. 1942. Rose marble, 15⅝ h. Lent by The Museum of Modern Art, New York; Gift of William S. Paley (by exchange), 1948. (ILLUS. P. 93)

100. *Charles Baudelaire.* c. 1940–45. Marble, 17 h. Lent by Hirshhorn Museum and Sculpture Garden, Smithsonian Institution, Washington, D.C. (ILLUS. P. 95)

101. *Group of Figurines.* c. 1940–45. Plaster or terra-cotta, 5¼ to 12¼ h. (ILLUS. PP. 98–99)

102. *Figure.* c. 1943–45. Gilt bronze, 11¾ h. Lent by Nelson A. Rockefeller, New York.

103. *Figure.* c. 1943–45. Gilt bronze, 12½ h. Lent by Nelson A. Rockefeller, New York.

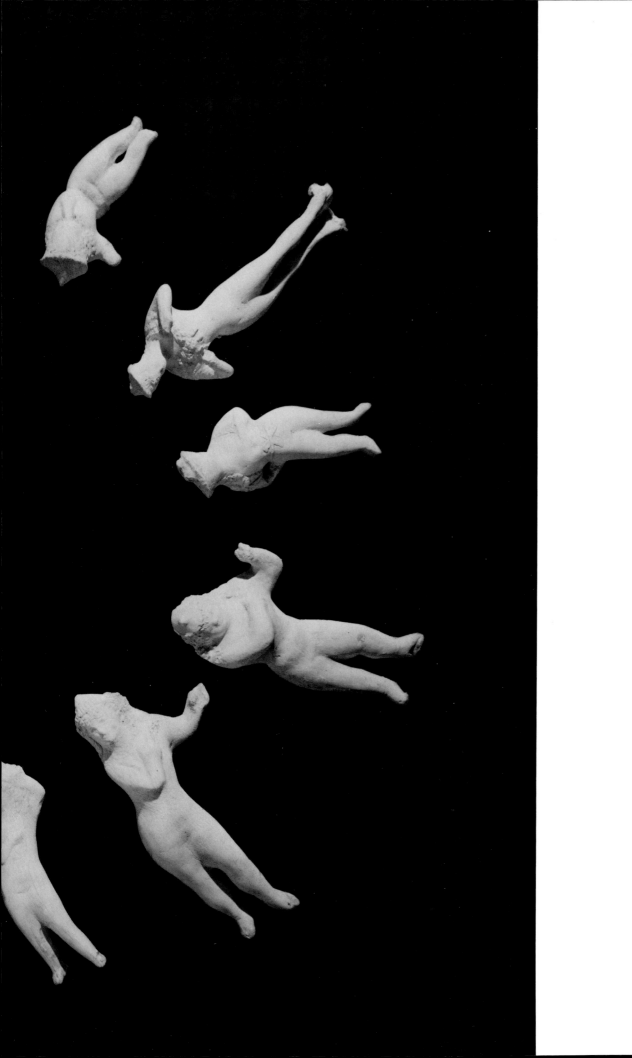

DRAWINGS

[104]

104. *Head and Neck.* c. 1905–06. Ink, 11⅛×7½. Lent by The Metropolitan Museum of Art, New York; Gift of Lincoln Kirstein, 1965. (ILLUS. P. 101)

105. *Head.* c. 1906. Ink, 16¼×11.

106. *Head of a Woman.* c. 1906? Pencil and ink, 16⅛×11⅜. Lent by The Museum of Modern Art, New York; Gift of Lincoln Kirstein in memory of Rene d'Harnoncourt.

107. *Standing Female Nude.* c. 1904–07. Ink, 19¾×8⅛. Lent by The Museum of Modern Art, New York; Gift of Lincoln Kirstein in memory of Rene d'Harnoncourt. (ILLUS. P. 104)

108. *Bird in Flight.* c. 1904–07. Ink, 8³⁄₁₆×12⁹⁄₁₆. Lent by The Metropolitan Museum of Art, New York; Gift of Lincoln Kirstein, 1965.

[105]

[108]

[106]

[107]

[109]

[110]

[111]

109. *Standing Female Nude*. c. 1904–07. Ink, 11⅜ × 5¼. Lent by The Baltimore Museum of Art; Gift of Mme Helena Rubinstein.

110. *Head*. c. 1904–07. Ink and wash, 6⅝ × 5½. Lent by The Museum of Modern Art, New York; Gift of Lincoln Kirstein in memory of Rene d'Harnoncourt.

111. *Head*. c. 1907. Ink, 16⅜ × 12¾. Lent by The Museum of Modern Art, New York; Gift of Lincoln Kirstein in memory of Rene d'Harnoncourt.

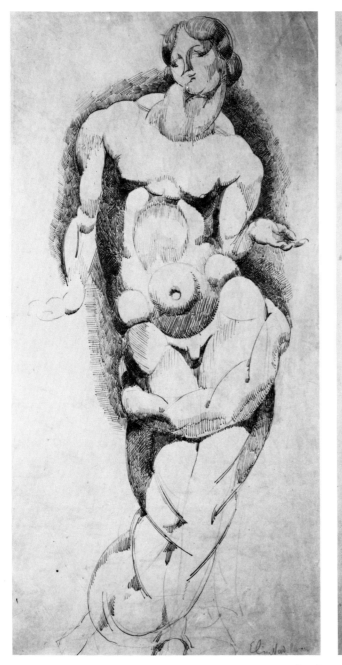

[113]

[114]

112. *Standing Nude.* c. 1907–08. Ink, 23¼× 10 (sight). (†)

113. *Standing Male Nude.* c. 1909. Pencil and ink, 21¾× 9¾. Lent by Hirshhorn Museum and Sculpture Garden, Smithsonian Institution, Washington, D.C.

114. *Standing Female Nude.* c. 1909. Ink and pencil, 21¾× 8¾. Lent by Hirshhorn Museum and Sculpture Garden, Smithsonian Institution, Washington, D.C.

115. *Caricature of a Man.* c. 1909? Ink, 15⅞× 11⅞. Lent by The Metropolitan Museum of Art, New York; Gift of Lincoln Kirstein, 1965.

116. *Head of a Woman.* c. 1907–10. Ink, 21× 12½. Lent by Albright-Knox Art Gallery, Buffalo, New York; Charles W. Goodyear Fund. (†)

117. *Head.* c. 1907–10? Ink and pencil, 17× 11½ (sight). (†)

118. *Standing Nude.* c. 1908–10? Ink, 13⅝× 7. Lent by Mr. and Mrs. Harry W. Anderson, Atherton, California.

[118]

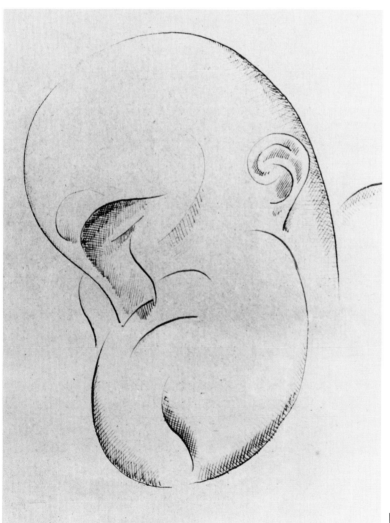

[115]

[119]

[120]

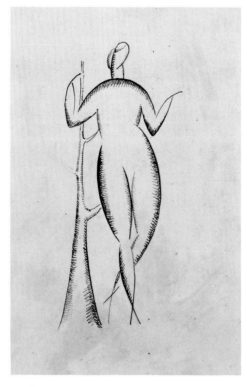

[121]

119. *Nude.* c. 1908–10? Ink, 22¼ × 10¼. Collection Whitney Museum of American Art, New York.

120. *Decorative Figure.* c. 1910. Ink, 20⅜ × 8⅞. Lent by Zabriskie Gallery, New York.

121. *Androgynous Figure Against a Tree Trunk.* c. 1909–11. Ink, 12⅝ × 8. Lent by Mr. and Mrs. Howard Sloan, New York.

122. *Male Nude.* 1908–12. Ink, 14 × 8⅜. Lent by Dey Gosse, New York.

[122]

[124]

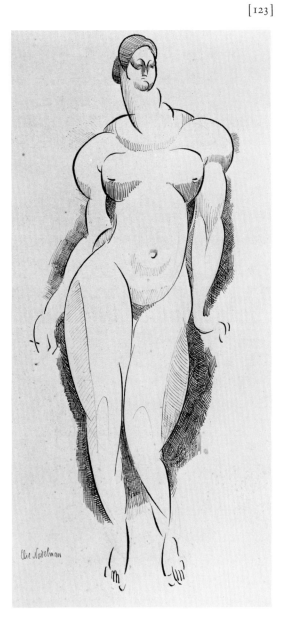

[123]

123. *Nude.* c. 1908–12. Ink, 19⅝ × 9½. Lent by Zabriskie Gallery, New York.

124. *Reclining Horse.* c. 1912. Ink, 8¼ × 10½. Lent by Mr. and Mrs. Maurice Vanderwoude, Great Neck, New York.

125. *Study for Autumn.* c. 1911–13. Chalk, 8¼ × 18½. Lent by The Metropolitan Museum of Art, New York; Gift of Lincoln Kirstein, 1965.

[129]

[125]

[126]

[127]

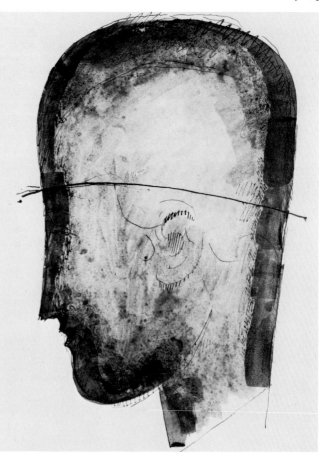

126. *Horse*. c. 1913–14. Pencil and ink wash, 7¾× 10½. Lent by The Baltimore Museum of Art; Blanche Adler Fund.

127. *Head of Man in the Open Air* (or *Profile of Man in Bowler Hat*). c. 1913–14. Ink and wash, 7× 5¾. Lent anonymously.

128. *Cow with Horns*. c. 1913–14. Pencil, ink and wash, 7¹¹⁄₁₆× 10¹⁄₁₆. Lent by The Metropolitan Museum of Art, New York; Gift of Lincoln Kirstein, 1965.

129. *Calligraphic Head*. c. 1914. Ink, 9× 5¾. (ILLUS. P. 111)

130. *Sketch of a Poodle*. c. 1914. Pencil, ink and wash, 7¹⁵⁄₁₆× 10¼. Lent by The Metropolitan Museum of Art, New York; Gift of Lincoln Kirstein, 1965.

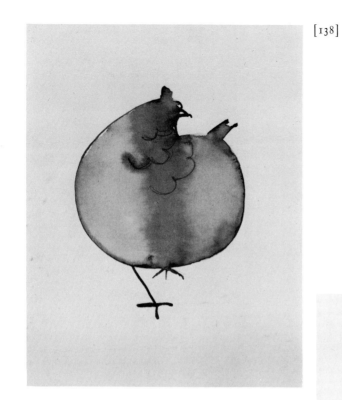

[138]

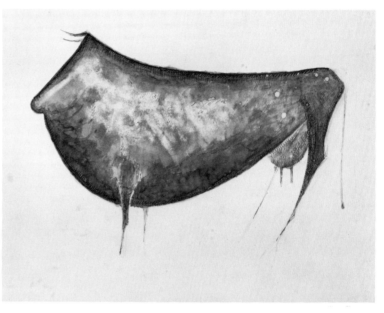

[128]

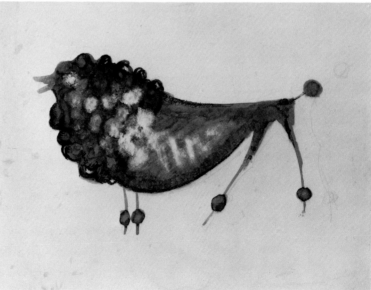

[130]

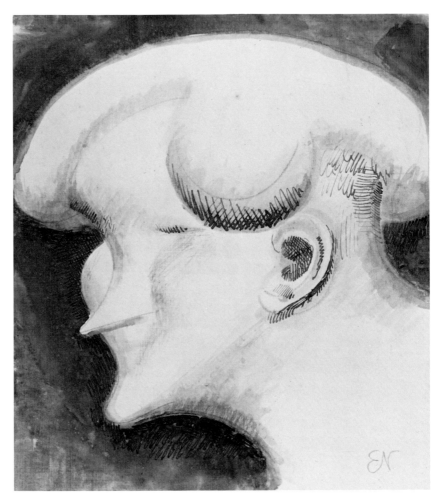

[134]

131. *Study for Man in the Open Air*. c. 1915. Watercolor and ink, 10⅞ × 7⅛. Lent by The Museum of Modern Art, New York; Aristide Maillol Fund.

132. *Kneeling Figure*. c. 1915. Ink, 14¾ × 15 (sight). Lent by Dey Gosse, New York.

133. *Tango*. c. 1915. Ink and wash, 12⅛ × 8¼. Lent anonymously. (†)

134. *Head*. c. 1917. Pencil, ink and wash, 8¼ × 7½.

135. *Study for Seated Woman*. c. 1917. Ink and wash, 9⅜₆ × 7½. Lent by Hirshhorn Museum and Sculpture Garden, Smithsonian Institution, Washington, D.C.

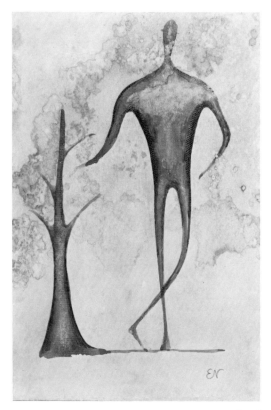

[131]

[135]

[132]

136. *Jazz Drummer.* c. 1915–18. Ink, 9×5¾. (†)

137. *Dancing Couple.* c. 1917–19. Ink and wash, 9⅞×8. Lent by The Metropolitan Museum of Art, New York; Gift of Lincoln Kirstein, 1965.

138. *Hen.* c. 1919. Ink and wash, 6½×5. Lent by Hirshhorn Museum and Sculpture Garden, Smithsonian Institution, Washington, D.C. (ILLUS. P. 113)

139. *Figure with Billowing Skirt.* c. 1919. Ink, 18¾×9½.

140. *Two Classical Draped Figures.* c. 1921. Ink, 9×6. Lent by Joseph H. Hirshhorn Private Collection, New York.

[137]

[140]

[139]

[141]

141. *Woman's Head.* c. 1920–22. Pencil, 9½×7⅛. Lent by Mr. and Mrs. Louis S. Myers, Akron, Ohio.

142. *Head of a Woman.* c. 1920–22. Ink and wash, 12½×8. Lent by The Museum of Modern Art, New York; Gift of Lincoln Kirstein in memory of Rene d'Harnoncourt.

143. *Equestrienne.* c. 1923–25. Ink, 9⅞×7¹⁵⁄₁₆. Lent by The Metropolitan Museum of Art, New York; Gift of Lincoln Kirstein, 1965.

144. *Profile of a Male Head (Self-Portrait?).* c. 1925. Pencil and wash, 10×8. Lent by Hirshhorn Museum and Sculpture Garden, Smithsonian Institution, Washington, D.C.

[142]

[143]

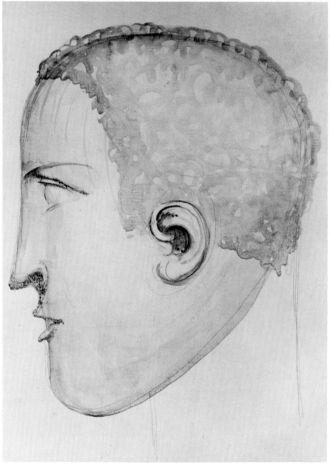

[144]

Design of catalogue by Joseph Bourke Del Valle
Design of New York exhibition by Arthur Clark
Design of Washington exhibition by Joe Shannon

Photographs by Geoffrey Clements, and E. Irving Blomstrann, Barney Burstein, John A. Ferrari, R. F. Ganley, Helga Photo Studio, Peter A. Juley & Son, Paulus Leeser, Martin Leifer, Mates-Katz, O. E. Nelson, Eric Pollitzer, Nathan Rabin, Walter Russell, John D. Schiff, Soichi Sunami, Eric Sutherland, William Suttle, Taylor and Dull, Charles Uht.

Composition by Press of A. Colish, Inc., Mount Vernon
Printing and binding by The Falcon Press, Philadelphia